T0110880

GROWING UP NAVY

COPING AND ADAPTING TO CHANGE

TREY'CE E. RICHARDSON

authorHOUSE®

AuthorHouse™
1663 Liberty Drive
Bloomington, IN 47403
www.authorhouse.com
Phone: 833-262-8899

Published by AuthorHouse 01/29/2021

ISBN: 978-1-6655-1549-8 (sc)
ISBN: 978-1-6655-1554-2 (e)

Library of Congress Control Number: 2021901656

CONTENTS

DEDICATION

For my late grandfather, Pierre Etienne Barnaba Jr. and grandmother, Michele Yvette Richardson, who were always supportive and inspirational throughout my life, giving me a significant 'push' to focus on the worthwhile goals while leaving everything insignificant behind. To imagine this short story without them would be impossible, as they were instrumental in getting me through the different episodes of my life. It would be true to say they also took an active part in the creation of this story, teaching me the importance of embracing and highlighting the most valuable moments of life.

PREFACE

The progression of writing was both fun and weird, as, sometime it was difficult to think of storylines while trying to recollect significant events from my earlier years, and then, focus on the ongoing current events. My parents encouraged me to remain devoted to the process of transforming my good and bad experiences into a testimony, which led to a promising objective—you know, like conquering a new level of a video game.

Based on my experiences of growing up in a dual military household, I wanted to share the following pages as my personal outlook of the world. It is my enriched perspective of moving to different places, and the influential imprints left on one's heart and mind. It is about the aspect of storytelling that military dependents seem to avoid for some reason, but which is so important to re-discovering the complex nature of relationships and the process of growing up from a 12-year-old African American male viewpoint. The practice of journaling this short story has resulted in my willingness to share my truth through the lens of living and getting through the coronavirus pandemic, followed by a social movement that rocked my generation. Along my journey, I had to finding a place of belonging, reuniting with childhood friends, progressing through school, and supporting my parents and their military obligations. Again, writing was both fun and weird, sometimes hard. Now that the book has come to fruition...I have to get back to the challenge of another new level of my favorite PlayStation 5 video game. Happy reading!

ACKNOWLEDGEMENTS

I would like to thank my mother and father for encouraging me early on to journal and capture my thoughts, feelings, and emotions in real-time. I have learned a lot about myself throughout the process and the best version of me I aspire to become. None of this would be possible without your unconditional love and support. I love you guys so much!

DISCLAIMERS

The information or material contained in this book, including advice and opinions, are the author's own and do not reflect endorsement by or the views of the United States Government, Department of Defense, or the United States Department of the Navy. The author is solely responsible and liable with respect to the content of this book. Although the words "he," "she," "him," "her," "his," and "hers," are used sparingly in this book to enhance communication, they are not intended to be gender driven nor to be an affront to or discriminate against anyone reading the text.

CHAPTER 1

Introduction

Hello, my name is Trey'ce Etienne Richardson. I know, what a unique name. I said the same thing when I first learned how to pronounce it. Although my family and close friends call me "Buddha", my mother coined that name because I was chunky and resembled the Great Buddha statue in Kamakura, Japan. I am blessed to have the name in honor of one of my dad's favorite Aunt's, Tracey Marlene; and my mom's dad, my Paw-paw, Pierre Etienne.

My parents decided to depart from the traditional name spelling, so they changed it to clarify that I was, in fact, a boy, not a girl. My Uncle Hendu and Aunt Steph added the apostrophe to my name for more distinction and so, the name Trey'ce was born. I am the proud son and perfect blend of Dennis and Shannan Richardson, baby brother to my two older sisters, Daz'sha and Cheyanne. I am an average twelve-year-old young man, of African American and French descent (Creole). I tend to stand out from the crowd because I am outspoken and charming. I sport a distinctive hairstyle, am blessed with a creative mind, and I enjoy making people laugh. In other words, I am often mistaken as "The Class Clown" by nearly ALL my teachers – minor misunderstanding, though, of course. I am still working to reduce the constant mischaracterization! Lol.

It is so cool being the youngest; I get away

with everything, well, almost everything, at least, I try to. My big sisters had to be kind to me, at least, when my parents were around. Lol. My oldest sister, Daz'sha, lives in Detroit, Michigan, with my nephew Dai'jon and works at Ford Motor Company. General Motors, Ford Motor Company and Fiat Chrysler are the largest car manufacturers in North America, also known as the Big Three. These three companies started out in Detroit, MI and have been a source of employment for the majority of my father's side of the family. It is a really good and important job to have – my family is so proud of her. So, I do not see my older sister and nephew very often because they live in another state. However, when they do come to visit, we have a lot of fun together. My oldest sister is terrible at Monopoly, like the absolute worst. Lol. It tickles me to watch her auction off her properties to pay my dad every dime she owes. Sure, I am usually the next person to go bankrupt but still – she usually leads the charge. I do wish they lived closer so I could see them more often, though. I miss them a lot. My other sister Cheyanne lives in Dallas, Texas, and is a senior at Baylor University studying to become an RN. Everybody calls her Chy except my Dad – he calls her Chy Boogie. Baylor University is nationally ranked and categorized with schools such as the University of Chicago and Carnegie Mellon University. Both of my sisters have done very well for themselves, and as a result, I have my work cut out for me to meet and or exceed the expectations that are now set out for me. We share a ten year age gap, but you would hardly notice if I did not disclose it. See, Chy and I have always had a unique way of communicating with each other. For instance, when I was younger, she would tell me that I was annoying, but that was just code for "I really really enjoy the quality time and creating precious memories with you, my handsome brother". And so, at her request, I would continue with whatever it was I was doing. Lol. I often got in trouble for mocking her, as well as invading her privacy whenever she had her friends over to visit, especially her first official boyfriend Matteo. It was hard for us to bond and really get along growing up simply because we were always at different stages of life; Chy was a teenager learning to drive, and I was still busy playing with Legos. I always wished we were a little closer in age so that we could have attended school together and experienced things at the same time. Although now, we get along much better, while she still says that I get on her nerves, I still maintain that I know what she really means. Lol.

As for my parents, well, they are both Active Duty Service Members serving in the United States Navy. My dad is a Commissioned Naval Officer and specializes in surface ship marine engineering; manages complex maintenance and repair of main propulsion, auxiliary and electrical machinery systems. My mom is a security professional, also known as a Master-At-Arms or "12"; responsible for safety and security (law enforcement and force protection) for surface ships and installations. As a minority female Master Chief, she is pretty much a Bad Mama Jama! As a result of these two awesome individuals, I was born on June 22, 2008, at Naval Medical Hospital in Yokosuka, Japan. It is the largest U.S. military treatment facility on the mainland Japan, near Tokyo. Pretty cool, huh? Unfortunately, I did not get the chance to live in Japan long enough to fully experience the culture and attend the Department of Defense (DoD) school like Chy. It was only daycare for me before my family completed their overseas duty tour and were ultimately reassigned to Naval Station Norfolk in Norfolk, Virginia -- the world's largest naval station coupled with the largest concentration of naval forces. By this time, Daz'sha was in the early stages of her career, financially independent, and living out her adulthood in Detroit, MI. So, naturally, Cheyanne's educational stability ahead of middle and high school would become my parent's top priority and driving factor to return to the United States. My parents decided to build a new construction house and settle in Chesapeake, Virginia area, where my sister and I now call home. Chesapeake is among the seven cities that include Portsmouth, Hampton, Newport News, Virginia Beach, Norfolk and Suffolk that make up the Hampton Roads area. I am a little bias, but Chesapeake is by far the best place to live; beautiful scenery, wonderful sense of community, and excellent schools. It was by far the best decision they ever made!

CHAPTER 2

Making new friends

I do not remember a lot of details of the time spent in Japan or my younger years. However, my memory seems to become a lot clearer when I think back to around five years old, when I first entered Kindergarten. I attended Greenbrier Primary School; great school full of awesome teachers and faculty committed to providing students like myself with the best education. It was here where I met my soon to be best friend, Cory; we call him CJ, since his name was given to him after his dad. It was like CJ and I were born to be best friends. He was tall, skinny, and very quiet – at least around our parents, but when it was just us alone, he was so funny and goofy; it was like a totally different person. His family, like mine, moved into the Eagle Lake at Plantation North in Chesapeake, Virginia. The only difference was that their move was local, and mine was international. Luckily for me, they moved into the house right next door, in the summer of 2010. The timing of their move couldn't have been any more perfect; finally, a kid who was the same age as me that I could play with in my cul-de-sac. The neighborhood would never be the same – power wheels, BMX bikes, skateboards, gas-powered mini-bikes and go-carts would litter public streets and neighbor's yards over the years. And getting into "Good Trouble" over the years was inevitable. I remember one time when we were 5 and 6 years old, we snuck into my sister Chy's shower and put Nair Hair Remover on our legs, thinking that it was one of her body lotions. Boy, oh, boy did we get in big trouble for that one! Needless to say, our families grew closer through our many shenanigans; my mom and his mom clicked like they were long lost sisters, and my dad was a perfect fit with his dad. CJ unknowingly joined a close family-oriented community.

Linden and Maxwell, my other close friends in the neighborhood, who happen to be brothers, lived down the street. Linden and Maxwell were so fun, and naturally, being brothers, they were very competitive with each other and always fought over who was the best at whatever it was they were doing, which was most enjoyable to watch. Linden was the quietest, but Maxwell was more outgoing of the two. It did not matter to me because being around them and their family made me wish I had a brother of my own to play and grow up with. But we had so much in common, and it was the next best thing to actually having a blood brother. I remember we had identical toy cars from the Pixar Disney Movie "CARS". I would always take mine down to their house so we could race them. I guess I must have forgotten that I took Lindens' car along with mine back home because my mom asked why I had two of the same cars. Little did I know, Mrs. Belinda, my other mom, had called and asked my mom to check for the missing car. Yup, I definitely had Linden's car. Needless to say, a formal shakedown became standard every time I would leave their house; Mr. Larry, my other dad, would pat all of us down to ensure no one was smuggling each other's toys. We all got a kick out of it. Lol. Even though none of us were blood-related, we always told people that we were real brothers, and they believed us. My sister Chy became good friends with their sister Brianna as well. I learned the importance of establishing and maintaining healthy relationships from my family early on. These relationships helped me to build trust and confidence as well as empowered me with an organic feeling of being supported by the people who were of the most importance in my life.

My fondest memory was how every year around the Thanksgiving and Christmas holiday, it would snow, and our dads would take us all to the steep hill in the neighborhood to go sledding. If the slopes were too crowded, our dads would improvise and attach a rope to the back of the truck and pull us around the cul-de-sac. I remember one year, my parents let Chy do the "snow challenge." It was where you would run out, jump in the snow, and make a snow angel wearing only a t-shirt and shorts. My parents would not allow me to do it because they said that I was still too young. One of these days, I will do it because those YouTube and TikTok challenges are hilarious to watch!

In the summers, when I had gotten a little older, my dad would let us ride our bikes to 7-11 to get ice cream; I would get the ninja turtle popsicle with the bubble gumball attached. It did not bother me how all that the ice cream made my lips turn blue – small price to pay for a bubble gumball. Lol. Permission to ride our bikes to 7-11 without an adult was conditional, though. I basically had to bribe my dad with an Oreo cookie sandwich. Now, bribing my mom was nearly impossible, so we avoided asking her at all cost, and if she was in ear-shot whenever I was sneakily asking my dad, a soft whisper was always the way to go. Lol. I loved our neighborhood; my friends were close enough that I could walk to their houses and play outside without fear. All the neighbors got along, and the adults would always look out for all the other kids. Since my house was located in a cul-de-sac, it became the default location for playing outside since it was safer and easier than playing in the street.

Over the next twelve years, I would repeat moving to new areas, including San Diego, CA, and back to Chesapeake, VA, making new friends, and creating lasting memories. It seems fun and exciting, but it was tough coping and adapting to constant change. However, I know, above all, a strong, resilient, and supportive family like mine is all I ever need to overcome any of the challenges I will face in life.

CHAPTER 3

Full Speed Ahead

When I started at Greenbrier Primary School, I felt so uncomfortable and awkward. Similar to those times, when you have to go with parents to one of their friend's houses, and you do not know anyone, including the adults who remind you of the times they used to change your diapers - awkward. Yes, I would pretend to remember these moments, even when I had no idea. Embarrassed is how I felt; on the first day of school in the United States.

I did not get the opportunity to experience pre-school (yochien) in Japan, only day nurseries (hoikujo) with other military kids born abroad. I missed the opportunity of making good friends like CJ, Linden, and Maxwell early on. After completing the first two years of grade school in Virginia, I started to adjust and better understand what my routine would be like, living as a military child. It was hard to accept. For example, neither my mom nor my dad had much time in the morning to be typical parents; wake me up, cook breakfast, and send me off to school. I mean, they had to wake up early and leave the house to make it to work on time themselves, so I was left to get on with it with the help of my older sister. I can count the days that they had the time to stay to make cereal or walk me to the bus stop. That was mostly left up to my sister Chy, and later my nanny, Mrs. Karen. Initially, the idea of a nanny made me feel like a baby, but I quickly grew to appreciate Mrs. Karen more and more the older I got. The comfort of knowing that I had another mother-like figure to count on without fail was so empowering. She was so good to me; helped me get ready in the morning and walked me to the bus stop for school. It genuinely felt like I had two moms. #Winning! I liked when Mrs. Karen brought her kids, Alyssa and Connor, over to my house, although I did not like having to share my toys with them. We would fight over them, and Mrs. Karen would always say "Sharing is Caring", which is one of the most valuable lessons that has become part of my character today. Now, I do not even mind sharing as it has become a learned behavior for me to compromise and encourage fairness.

I did not fully understand why I had a nanny until my dad had to leave for an extended period of time. He went on deployment that lasted for nearly a year. Deployment is a term used by the military and describes the movement of personnel, in this case, Sailors from their primary duty station to a destination outside the U.S. In the Navy, a deployment usually lasts between 6 to 12 months, depending on whether the deployment is a part of a foreign war or a peaceful mission. Nonetheless, I still felt sad because I did not fully understand what was happening; and why my dad had to leave us and was always away from home. None of my friend's Dads were leaving them for so long. All I knew was that one day, my dad was here, and the next, he was gone and no longer around or available for my sisters and me. My mom would make us write letters, send cards, and boxes full of his favorite snacks to stay connected with him while he was away. I remember asking her, "how do you know if he receives all the things we send?" She replied, "he is greedy and always asking for more!" Knowing this helped me pass the time when my dad was gone but, more importantly, helped me understand that my parents were trying to provide me with balance and consistency in their stead. Mrs. Karen represented that consistency and prevented any disruption in my comforting balance.

One of the best days ever was when he returned from a nine-month deployment. Even though I started crying when I saw him, I was so happy my best friend was finally back home. I did not realize that whenever my dad got deployed on a new ship, I lost focus, and my ability to exercise self-control in school dwindled. After one or two months of his absence, I would start to get in trouble a little, and unfortunately, that is how teachers got to know my name and who I was. The feeling of worry and uncertainty would be my experience and pattern for many more years to come as a military child. My older sister Chy was unable to comfort me because she had grown numb to the absence of mom and dad for extended periods of time, but for me, this was new and extremely difficult to understand and handle. With there being a ten year age gap between my sister and me, she had already experienced the emotions and struggles of being a military child. Even worse, she had to live with our grandparents for the first two years of her life while our parents were assigned to combatant warships. I am so grateful to my parents for making the necessary career adjustments to prevent this from ever happening again when I was born. I could not even begin to imagine the separation anxiety Chy had to endure. At least I was able to remain connected to my parents through email, phone calls and facetime, but none of these options were available to Daz'sha and or Chy during the earlier years of their life. They were restricted to letter mail only. OMG – I would've died of extreme anxiety!

My dad and I have the best father-son relationship. He has always been a great teacher and role model; took the time to create memorable father-son moments, render support and dissect my missteps to ensure I understood the second and third order effects. Even when I disappointed my parents, my dad and I still remained the best of friends. I would always ask, "Are we still best friends?" when he was mad at me, and he would always respond, "absolutely, son". It was in these moments, I knew my parents loved and prioritized nothing ahead of our well-being. It has always been okay to make an honest mistake in my family. However, my parents were very clear that it was completely unacceptable to make the same mistake twice. My parents interpreted that as a clear indication that we didn't learn from the miscue and parental intervention was necessary. And every intervention was methodical and intended to leave a lasting impression – SMH, I get chills thinking about some of those moments. Lol.

Transitioning from one country to another, one state to another, and adjusting to my parents' absence became the new norm for me. I think I began to feel some sense of normalcy around the 3rd or 4th grade. I met many people, and my support system expanded. At one point, I had more than 50 friends, although some were fake. Either way, it was a fantastic experience, but I did not care much about their "fake friendship." See, some friends are better than none. If I could remember, most of my real friends in 3rd grade outside of my brothers were;

Noah, Robert, Christan, Gabriel, Bryce, and Ronnie. Not all, but a large number of the rest were "counterfeit", meaning fake friends, as my mom would often refer to them as. Since I did not live in close proximity to my extended family in Detroit and Oklahoma, the term friends took on an entirely different meaning. My close friends became cousins, and my parent's friends became aunts and uncles. Because of the dynamics of being a military child, my friendships are very sacred to me. I recognize that in the absence of these meaningful friendships, I would have been extremely vulnerable to some really serious emotional trauma that might have changed my trajectory.

CHAPTER 4

May I have another, please!

I was so naive to think deployments only occurred once per military family throughout their career. When my dad returned, I assumed that dreadful experience would be no more, and I would never have to experience that pain and sense of abandonment again. Well, I couldn't have been more wrong. It was not long before my mom, this time, was tasked to deploy for seven months. She was stationed onboard USS ARLINGTON (LPD 24), an amphibious transport dock ship named for Arlington County, Virginia, the location of the Pentagon and crash site of American Airline Flight 77 during the terrorist attack on September 11, 2001. The excruciating pain I felt when my dad deployed was harsh, but the absence of my mom was *HORRENDOUS*! I don't care what anyone says, there is no one like your mom. I remember the weekend before she had to deploy, my mom, Chy and I were laying in Chy's bed watching the movie, "The Visit." Probably shouldn't been watching that movie at such a young age, but oh well. Anyway, at the end of the movie, I remember making my mom and sister laugh so hard because I was dancing to all the eerie songs like I knew them. We all laughed so hard, and somehow, I felt that everything would be okay when my mom left us.

It's never easy knowing that one of your parents is not going to be home for a while and just like when my dad was gone, I needed to find new coping mechanisms that would help me escape the feeling of loneliness. In coping, I would sleep on her side of the bed every night until she returned. In the morning, before getting out of bed, I would take a deep sniff of her pillow, then reach over and grab her iPad and listen to our favorite song, "Don't Wake Me Up," by Chris Brown. I took showers in her bathroom and used her soap so I could have her scent. All these things would be so necessary to manage my anxiety. Unlike when my dad deployed, my mom was always around to help through tough times of his absence. However, with mom gone, things became pretty tricky because my dad was great, but he wasn't mom. Not even close. Mom made delicious home-cooked meals every day with sides and desserts. As for my Dad, well…he was struggling and coping with the absence of my mom, too. He could not keep it together. Lol. The purpose and power of prayer had never been more important until my mom deployed and my Dad was left in charge. Lol. He would either order food, overcook meals in the crockpot, or make quick frozen meals in the microwave. Thank goodness my sister could cook. Mom always helped me with my homework, but my dad did make it much more fun and did a lot of funny things to help me remember and or pay attention to whatever it was I had to learn that week. It took Dad a while to get into the swing of things and to perfect our routine, but I appreciated everything he did for my sister and me. We were just totally unprepared for a scenario that featured dad as our primary care provider……"Lawd Have Mercy!". Lol.

The deployment finally ended, and my

mom returned safe and sound. The best part of my parent's deployment was when it was time for their homecomings. This time, my mom surprised me at school in front of my entire class. It is was magical. Everyone cheered, and I could not hold back the tears and she couldn't either. Boy, oh boy, my buddies teased me about it for a very long time, but I did not care because it was impossible to hold back those emotions after not seeing my mom for so long. Plus, they were incapable of understanding the significance of the moment as they didn't have to go without their mom for long periods of time like I did.

Fast forwarding to when I was nine years old, I remember when my parent's convened a family meeting. During that meeting, they broke the news that we were moving to San Diego, CA, for their next assignment. My sister had graduated from high school; and would be attending Baylor University during this time. My oldest sister was in Michigan, so that meant I would be moving by myself without any of my siblings for support. I know that one might say, don't you have a phone, iPad, computer etc.... to FaceTime, text and call. However, electronics don't take the place of having your sisters, family and friends physically there to share the unknowns with you. I recalled this news with nostalgia. I was happy for both my sisters as they now had their own lives to live. On the other hand, however, I was sad I had to leave my friends behind, my "brothers", my neighborhood, and all that I had grown so close to over the years. Because of this experience, I vowed never to join the military and subject my kids to the life of being a military child. I am not for sure if I could ever be as strong as my parents. I can only imagine what they go through mentally and emotionally every day when they put on their uniforms. I will always render honors to our service members for their courage to be brave and strong for those that can't, and I am especially appreciative of the sacrifices that my parents made for our family and our country, but I want to change the generational cycle. Honoring my parent's sacrifices translates to me never putting my kids through the emotions and trauma of being separated from family to support orders of the military.

CHAPTER 5

Shifting My Rudder

The time came to move to San Diego, CA and when we finally did, it was strange and odd. I felt weird. A familiar feeling that I had endured when I first started school in Virginia for the first time, but even worse. I remember flying into San Diego and looking out the airplane window that overlooked the mountains. I did not know what to expect, but I knew that everything would somehow be okay. When we arrived in San Diego, we had to stay at the Navy Lodge; an official government lodging hotel for families transitioning to the area. Our room was huge with two queen beds, a TV, and a large balcony with a fascinating view. The vibe was absolutely amazing; there were multiple beaches, beautiful palm trees everywhere, and the weather was perfect. It was love at first sight. Now, I was really curious about what our newly built home was going to look like after we left the Navy Lodge.

My parents were building an urban-inspired condominium in the heart of South San Diego. It was convenient for shopping, the movie theater, and my school would be within walking distance from our new neighborhood. That meant no riding public school buses again. #Winning! When we walked into our new house, I was so disappointed. It was extremely small and a noticeable downgrade from our 3,000 square foot single family home in

Chesapeake, Virginia to a 1,800 square foot condominium. It wouldn't be long before I started missing the big backyard and cul-de-sac at my previous home where I could play and ride my bike or motorized go-cart without fear of being hit by a car. On the bright side, since my sister left for college I gained a dedicated game room in addition to my own bedroom. A couple of months of us settling in our new home, I met my neighbor Robert, who we call RJ. He was three years younger and would quickly become the little brother that I always wished I had. I would pick him up after school and walk him home. It was so cool. We played basketball, baseball, kick ball, soccer and even took family trips together. RJ was fascinated with Beyblades, so I gifted him mine and bought new ones for him for his birthday. We became the best of friends, spending most of our summer together playing outside until the streetlights came on. Then school resumed. The schools in San Diego were nearly, "all year round." And we had to wear uniforms. OMG - I hated wearing uniforms because they limited my creativity and, more importantly, my "drip". The school dress code did not allow me to really express my inner self; I hated looking like everyone else, I much preferred to stand out. We could only wear the shoes of our choice, but it wasn't enough for me. School uniforms are boring, and they suck! I did enjoy attending school in Southern California since they had an outdoor architectural design and feel. All the hallways and corridors were outside, and that was really cool. Our teachers encouraged us to take breaks as needed, so we could take a short walk to the bathroom or around the school for some fresh air. The lunch cafeteria and recess area were both outside as well, it hardly ever rained in Southern California – it was just beautiful weather all year around.

However, while my friends back in Virginia were enjoying a long summer break. I was still attending school. It seemed like we went to school all-year around without traditional breaks and going to school during these periods got on my nerves. It was pretty safe to say that I was really irritated! I understand studies have found that students lose about 27 percent more of their learning gains in the summer months but there has to be another way to recover those losses without sacrificing our much-needed time off. Well, I was joining fourth grade, and extremely nervous about the first day. The night before school, I could not sleep…I kept thinking…Will the kids talk to me? Like me? Will they want to fight me? The school I attended was diverse with many different cultures, like; Hispanic, Filipino, Asian, and Chinese. No one race or ethnic group make up a majority of California population but more than 41 percent of people in San Diego speak non-English languages, mostly Spanish. Sometimes teachers and students would blend dialogues, talk in English, then Spanish. It was confusing and difficult to blend into such a diverse classroom. However, I made a lot of cool friends while I was there, and I gained the experience of meeting people from all different kinds of backgrounds. Something I had not experienced much in Virginia. The benefit of meeting new people and furthering my understanding of different cultures was great. I also got to learn about their different beliefs and values. One of the most memorable friendships that forged through my experience was with Amir. I met Amir through a mutual friend, Jaden. Amir did not like me at first because he didn't really know me, plus I was the new kid in school but we became good friends due to our mutual interest in video games, especially Grand Theft Auto.

I was completely dumbfounded after learning that I had a male teacher. Most of my teachers in Japan and Virginia were female. It turns out, Mr. C would become my all-time favorite and best teacher ever. I remember one time when I was involved in an incident with my classmates that triggered a big fight and near suspension. The fight began after a Hispanic kid called me a derogatory name in reference to the color of my skin. Against everything my parents had imparted, I thought it was only fair to hurl a derogatory name back to him. Boy oh boy, was I wrong in thinking that. He told his other Hispanic friends what I said, and it was on! I found myself quickly surrounded with no way out. One of his friends pushed me, so I pushed him back and then a complete brawl erupted on the playground. Fists were flying everywhere. I was in the fight of my life; six against one. Mr. C emerged and pulled me from the rubble, and it felt like he had parted the Red Sea. He saved my life and outright earned the title "Best Teacher" ever. Lol.

Everyone involved learned and grew a lot from that incident. We realized that the use of derogatory epithets was wrong and can hurt people beyond our innocent intent of joanin' on each other. Did I mention that my mom and dad did not take too kind to my behavior? Whew, that's a chapter for my memoir entitled "The Art of Discipline". Future best seller. Lol.

CHAPTER 6

Welcome to 6ᵗʰ grade

Seems like the summer after finishing
the fifth grade flew by because we only
had a month and half break not like other
traditional schools that practically have
three months off. I do remember going to
Six Flags, LEGOLAND, and Aquatica Water
Park in that very short time. I had a blast at
all the theme parks. I loved LEGOLAND the
best. It has more than 60 rides, entertainment
shows and Lego attractions. To see almost
everything in the park made out of Lego's

was so cool. I have a collection myself that I started building when I was six year's old. The biggest one I built had over 2,000 pieces on it. Spending that time with my mom and dad was the best as we didn't always enjoy life as a family because one parent would be away with the military.

Needless to say, school was starting back and I had zero concerns. I was in the most senior class because Ocean View Hills School was an elementary school, grades K-6. I felt like I was the big man on campus. It also felt good to know that I would have a graduation ceremony and move on to the seventh grade. I was well-known and liked throughout the school. I was used to wearing uniforms by now and would put a lot of thought into making sure my socks and shoes matched the color polo shirt I had on and my hoodie for whenever it got a little chilly. Before my mom would leave for work, I would always ask my mom what level "drip was I on?" She would just laugh at me and say, "What kind of drip can you have wearing a uniform?" She never understood. LOL!

Most of my friends were returning and I was hoping that we would all get to be in the same class. When it came to the first day of school, I was worried when my friends told me that they were not sure about their class, but in a twist of fate, we were all together once again. However, it did not last long. After about one week into the school year, the school administrators started talking about how there were too many students in Mr. Sherman's and Ms. Bernard's class. Hence, they hired a new teacher named Ms. Mayor to create another classroom. As fate would have it, most of my friends were relocated to the new class. We had to get used to not being in the same class anymore, but we did have fun during lunchtime, recess, walking to the ice cream truck after school, and at home throughout the school year.

I was excited to find out that I was getting another male teacher because it eased my anxiety about grasping new concepts for all my classes. Mr. Sherman would make math and science fun as he would challenge our minds using real world events and not just use the traditional chalk board and textbook method that a lot of teachers often used. I felt that I had matured throughout my time at Oceanview Hills and could handle just about any situation that might come my way. Even though sixth grade was starting off great there was also so much drama with rumors, fights, and name-calling, but I had my best friend Amir through the whole time. I was in so many incidents, whether directly or indirectly, during my fourth and fifth grade year, the last thing I want to hear was my parent's mouth about how I was supposed to act in school and how I was supposed to treat people. I have to say, I starting understanding what they would constantly tell me, "to treat people how you want to be treated."

By the time the fall and winter breaks came around, I was getting more and more anxious about graduating because that meant time was getting closer to me getting back to Virginia. Over my winter break, I went on a seven day cruise with port visits to Ocho Rios and Cayman Islands. I really enjoyed this cruise because my sister Chy and my Maw-Maw, AKA Grandma, both went with us. There were so many activities on board the ship; arts and crafts, swimming pool, spa, gym, arcades, play productions, etc. However, just like the average military family, we were all in different states trying to fly and meet each other in Miami, Florida. My mom and I were in California, my dad was already in Virginia, my sister was in

Texas, and my Maw-Maw lived in Oklahoma. Eventually, we all made it to Miami, and it was the best trip ever. Out of the two places I visited, I would have to say I enjoyed Jamaica the most because I got to get on jet-ski's and eat some really good food. My sister Chy was scared to ride a jet-ski by herself but my dad and I peer-pressured her into riding alone. Lol. But she didn't go fast at all; straight up chicken. As always though, as long as my whole family were together, I was happy because it wasn't very often where we all had the chance to take trips together.

CHAPTER 7

ALL STOP – COVID 19 pandemic

Heading back to school after the winter break, I was telling myself that sixth grade was a breeze, along with having fun with my friends, and exciting new subjects of study. A couple months later all heck broke loose. A strange virus, later identified as the Corona Virus Disease - Twenty Nineteen (COVID-19), which might have originated in Wuhan, China, spread fast like a brushfire. A national pandemic is defined as an outbreak of a particular disease that spreads across several counties and affects a large number of people. And so, everyone, national leaders, our state and local officials, and teachers alike were in full panic mode. It was like a re-creation of the "Contagion," movie I watched a while ago when I moved to San Diego. It was not long before the principal announced that Ocean View Hills School would close indefinitely to safeguard against COVID-19.

Everyone was cheering and was excited, but little did we know we would soon have to deal with all of our schoolwork being online. It was hard because my teachers overwhelmed us with homework assignments as officials scrambled to develop a comprehensive recovery plan. I almost gave up, but I could almost hear my dad voice saying, "visualize, focus and execute." I successfully passed the sixth grade and was advanced to the seventh grade.

Due to National Security concerns of COVID-19 and effects on Military readiness, my mother had to return to Naval Air Station (NAS) North Island to provide security and implement force protection measures for the base. NAS North Island is located at the north end of Coronado peninsula on San Diego Bay; home port of several aircraft carriers. My dad was stationed back in Virginia again, but this time at Joint Expeditionary

Base Little Creek, closer to the worst-hit areas like; New York, New Jersey, and Philadelphia. An executive order was issued by President Donald J. Trump, directing all public, private, and charter schools to close until further notice. At first, with my limited knowledge, it felt like we were being given an early summer break. However, the reality soon hit me that this may be a long, agonizing, and lonely experience on top of being separated from my dad once again.

For a while, it felt like we were safe in San Diego from COVID-19, but oh boy, I was wrong once again. The numbers of people that were becoming infected kept steadily increasing, with the death toll reaching over 4,000 people in California. No one, myself included, is safe anymore. I could not help but worry about my dad, whose job was designated as "Essential", traveling into high-risk areas, inspecting naval warships.

My once adorable little neighborhood had turned into a haunted village. People no longer shook hands. I could not go outside and play with my friends, not even Aaden, a close neighbor.

The COVID-19 pandemic disrupted not only my life but also the entire world's system. World economies were crumbling, and both health and education systems were fast failing. Food that was in plenty were fast becoming scarce. Additionally, essential household goods such as toiletries, fruit snacks, and cereals were starting to become hard to find in the convenience stores. The other day, we went to do some shopping, and could hardly get all the essential items that we needed. I overheard two adults complaining and saying that some people overbought these crucial commodities out of panic. People all over San Diego and the world are not sure when the pandemic would end. A vaccine is our only hope at this point!

To add salt to the injury, my dad left me a voice message the other day about my granddad's untimely illness. A healthy and vibrant Granddad is no more. It was painful. In the short message Dad left, I learned that Granddad had possibly contracted COVID-19 in Detroit, where my dad's side of the family resided. To say I was shocked would be an understatement. I cried. I wailed.

Furthermore, the memories we all shared flashed through my mind, most painfully, as if I would soon bid him goodbye. I could see Granddad's grin sheepishly, as he took all the grandkids to the store to buy whichever ice cream we wanted. His illness has been devastating, and for the first time, I felt like I was losing another "Father-Like Figure." I also started to think of my "Maw Maw" who lives by herself in Del City, Oklahoma;

a suburban city within the Oklahoma City metropolitan area. I was wondering how she was maintaining through this pandemic. You see, she is still vibrant in her late 60's as she still enjoys the gym, going to church, and hunting in the woods. I was worried that she would be in the same boat as my Granddad and at-risk to contract COVID-19 virus due to her innocent exposure to someone that was unknowingly infected. Luckily for me, and for her, she is in pretty good health and is not as stubborn as my Granddad. I only have two grandparent's left and I would love to see them stay around just a little bit longer. I never had the chance to grow up like most kids being around their family because of my parent's career. I cherished every chance I got to see my grandparents.

As I sit here in my room, glancing out the window and looking at the sky, I cannot help but wonder what will happen to my education, life, and dreams. Will I achieve my goals and aspirations in life? Or will my young life snap away in a matter of seconds? How about my mom and dad? Will they come back safely? Tough questions that only time can answer.

CHAPTER 8

How COVID-19 affected me

This pandemic has been the most annoying thing that has ever happened in my life. I do not know why the World Health Organization, Chinese government, and other entities, did not do more to protect us against the COVID-19 transmission and dissemination to the United States of America.

After the pandemic's ravages, my parents

would not allow me to play with my friends, including Aaden, who wanted to play with me all the time. My mom said that there was a need to keep socially distance from each other, which meant playing together was impossible. The instruction must have come from my dad. He had learned of children infections through CNN and Fox News network that most of the children were infected through playing together. He must have told my mother not to allow me to play with any of my friends to be on the safe side.

The fact that I could not play with my friends was terrible but being confined in the house was so much worse. My mother, who was the only adult at home with me, made sure that I never left the house after my dad expressed his concern. The rise of infections and deaths due to COVID-19 had now given everybody a scare, including my mother, a military woman, in law enforcement, who was used to significant dangers and practically fearless. It was so unfortunate that my movements would be monitored by her all the time.

I had no other choice but to subject myself to spending time in front of the television watching cartoons and playing video games. But that was short lived. My dad would call daily and make me look up current events, share COVID-19 articles, watch educational YouTube channels, which would inform us of mandatory face coverings, sanitizing our hands, avoiding public gathering, coughing into our flexed elbow, and maintaining social distance. The education system had faded into oblivion with most teachers who were enthusiastic about sending us homework all falling silent. My desire to go back to school to play with my friends remained just that, 'a desire.' I did not know how to move forward, since those who could provide the answer to when things would go back to normal were also dumbfounded, not knowing the next step of action.

It was more worrying that our usual way of life would soon change with crime being on the rise. We were waking up to the news that people were mugging others, looting, and vandalizing. Many young people were looking for something to keep them going since the economy was hit hard and most people had lost their jobs. The crime alone increased fear in me. Though I knew I had the protection of a well-trained military woman with a law enforcement background, my question is, what if they come in large numbers to my neighborhood? This concern was the ricocheting matter in my mind that gave me no peace.

My life had turned upside down. We could not go anywhere. I could not go to places like Dave n Busters, Jump Around, or even the barbershop. The thing that made me somewhat happy was that McDonald's drive-through was still open.

At least I could still order my favorite meal, number nine combo; a double cheeseburger with only ketchup, and a sprite. Even though I still had to do my schoolwork online, I was able to see my friends and teachers via Zoom video calls. Although the number of teachers and pupils on zoom was also reducing each day. I was still able to play online games with all my friends on my PlayStation game console, which was fun. I assume that by the time we were to move back to Virginia in the summer, the world would be in better shape, no more 'COVID-19'. Needless to say, THAT WAS NOT THE CASE!

It was extremely hard for me to acclimate to the change much less understand different mandates from California and Virginia. I had more freedom in California. There was so much misinformation about the virus that out of an abundance of caution, my parents decided to implement their own stay-at-home order even though the Governor of Virginia had officially lifted it months ago. And just like that, what was old was new again – COVID 19 was changing my life again. I will explain more of this throughout Chapter 9.

As if the COVID-19 pandemic was not bad enough, police brutality also revealed its ugly head when George Floyd was mercilessly killed. George Floyd was a 46-year-old African American who died on May 25, 2020 after being handcuffed and pinned to the ground by a police officer, who pressed his knee down onto his neck, cutting off his air supply. It was really sad to see the videos of him begging for his life when the police officer was suffocating him. Even more shocking, other police officers starred and kept guard as life slowly oozed out of Mr. Floyd. I asked myself if my mom, who works in military law enforcement, would ever do such a thing to person. That's when I knew what I witnessed was wrong and unacceptable.

Mr. Floyd's murder revealed the lack of accountability in the police sector, with many cases where African Americans were killed without any reason. The senseless killing of unarmed/innocent human being, regardless of ethnicity had to end, and so the social movement and demonstration began to take course. The mass campaign was spontaneous. Throughout the United States, it was clear that people were very angry with the police. As people demonstrated with poster boards in support of Black Lives Matter, they insisted an explanation and formal charges from the Minneapolis Police Chief. Specifically, they wanted immediate action taken against the police officers who were responsible for George Floyd's death. The demands for action through peaceful protest and demonstration went against the health directives of social distancing and wearing face coverings.

I had to ask my parents what they felt about all this; their words were sad and full of grief. My mom could not understand why a police officer who has sworn to uphold the constitution, and ensure the safety and quality of life of the communities he/she serve, would do this to a person. She believed that the people were right in demanding justice, which was long overdue not only to the African Americans but also to all victims of injustice.

My mom explained that the demonstrations were intended to call for respect for human life without looking at the color of the skin or ethnicity. Human life mattered, and nobody had the right to take it away. The looting that is done by some of those people who pretend to be demonstrators is something that shows that not all are in that movement in search of true justice, but rather, to gain from the death of Floyd by looting other people's property, burning down buildings, barricading section of cities, and inciting chaos and fear. All the fighting, protests, and violent demonstrations made me feel like the pandemic was over, and things were finally getting back to where they were before COVID 19 arrived from China.

CHAPTER 9

Returning to Homeport

Even though I knew there was turmoil and chaos surrounding me, all I could focus on was returning back to Virginia with the hope of life returning to some level of normalcy. I remember getting up really early to catch the flight back to Virginia, but I didn't care. After almost a whole day of flying, I started to get "butterflies" in my stomach when we landed back in Virginia because I knew that this would be the last time that I would have to move. The crew,

Linden and Maxwell, along with their mom, Mrs. Belinda, greeted us at Norfolk International Airport, which was a surprise to me. I was so happy. We talked in the truck all the way home, catching up on old times.

Even though we would be staying in an apartment for a few months, because our house was still under construction, I didn't care because I knew I was finally where I called "home". Life wasn't so bad in the apartment because I had a TV and my PlayStation 4 in my room, however, sleeping on the air mattress was like sleeping on the ground but I soon got used to it. LOL! I had hoped the swimming pool at the apartment would open soon, because it was summertime and I love to swim but with COVID-19 cases rising again, I didn't get my hopes up. That's when I thought to myself, "I cannot wait until we move into our new house." I had never lived in an apartment before and was totally grateful to have had a place to live but the people living in the apartment above us were loud, and nerve-racking. All I could do was find something to drown out the noise but oftentimes, I wasn't successful in doing so.

On the other hand, my birthday was fast-approaching but due to the pandemic, I spent my 12th birthday sitting around in the apartment for most of the day. I opened my gifts from my parents, sisters, and friends. I got some champion apparel and PlayStation network cards. I am allergic to saving, see, since money is combustible and could potentially catch fire and burn through my pockets, out of abundance of caution I try to spend it in a matter of minutes and hours. My parents were not happy about that, that's for sure. They are always telling me that I think money grows on trees or something. I admit, I need to do better at saving my money or cards for later, in case there is something I need. Plus, I never want to hear my dad's corny rhyme ever again….. "You can spend it fast or you can spend it slow but when it's gone, you ain't getting no mo'!"

Even though my birthday started out

boring, I later went to see the squad; CJ, Linden, and Maxwell; "the brothers from other mothers." Although playing in a hot facemask was tough; I knew we all had to wear them to help prevent the spread of the virus. Being in a pandemic, moving back to Virginia, missing my friends in California, had all taken a toll on my spirits. It was like an emotional roller coaster.

I thought the worst was behind me, but now, the world is even more chaotic due to the pandemic and the unfortunate incident surrounding the tragic death of George Floyd. Never would I have imagined that I would see buildings being burned down, protests and riots breaking out, people looting, and many other evils. Although our family was back whole, once again, my dad had to travel in this turmoil, and faced unknown's adversity. Feeling the loneliness of being a military child without one of my parents around seems all too familiar. After the unrest, my dad returned, and I soon realized the military put more stringent measures in place due to COVID-19 surge, coming back around in full force. You guessed it. Once again, we cannot go anywhere as a family; no nonessential stores, no beaches, no malls, and no travel beyond 50 miles. It feels like I am in the military at times because when my parents cannot do something, it affects me as well. In response to an increase in COVID-19 cases, the Department of Defense instituted broad measures to protect service members (e.g., mom and dad). We were directed to maintain physical distance of at least six feet from others whenever we were in close contact for fifteen (15) or more minutes and to always wear face coverings. It also prevented us from being involved in off-base activities such as recreational swimming pools, gyms, fitness facilities, barbershops, cinemas/theaters, dine-in restaurants, sporting events, public celebrations, beaches, and amusement parks — basically, WE CAN'T DO ANYTHING FUN!

Before I knew it, it was time for school to start. I was used to virtual learning as I got a good taste of it while in San Diego. Little did I know it was going to be quite different this time around. At first, we were logging in certain times of the day and week then before you know it, we were in virtual learning like we were in school. I thought to myself, I would rather just be in school. LOL! Then it came to a point where my school opened up for the opportunity to attend school on certain days while still being virtual on all the others. Little did I know, my parents had decided to sign me up for this option. I didn't know what to expect as I had to catch the bus to school, did not know where my classes were, where would I eat lunch, whether I would meet new friends, and the most important thing was, "would my drip" be on point. I can hear my mom now saying, "Your grades better have as much drip as your clothes." Needless to say, it all turned out better than I could have ever imagined.

However, I do believe my 12 years of experience as a military child gave me a lot of courage. I have learned to be very fluid, strong in times of uncertainty, respectful, open-minded, and patient. In my mind, I think I have endured and conquered more than most kids my age have over the years. I pride myself in knowing that no matter what happens in my lifetime, I have a strong foundation and the best examples that set me up for great success. It's just up to me to take the wisdom and apply it.

Happily, as I look back, I do not think I would change anything during my journey. I met people I would have never otherwise met, lived in various places, grew into my personality, developed an extended military family, and matured into a responsible and respectable young man. So, even when you think as a military child, life is chaotic; think of the positives and enjoy the ride! I can promise, you will never find another ride like it!

Printed in the United States
By Bookmasters